The Things We See

Written by Chemise Taylor

Illustrated by Alexis B. Taylor

Copyright © 2022 by My Skills Books

Published by My Skills Books

All rights reserved. No part of this publication may be reproduced, distributed, or transmitted in any form or by any means, including photocopying, recording, or other electronic or mechanical methods, without the prior written permission of the publisher, except in the case of brief quotations embodied in critical reviews and certain other noncommercial uses permitted by copyright law.

First Printing, 2022.

ISBN: 978-1-951573-47-8

www.myskillsbooks.com

Apple

Bed

Bench

Bird

Paper

Shirt

Book Bag

Bread

Car

Carrot

Cat

Chair

Coffee

Couch

Crayons

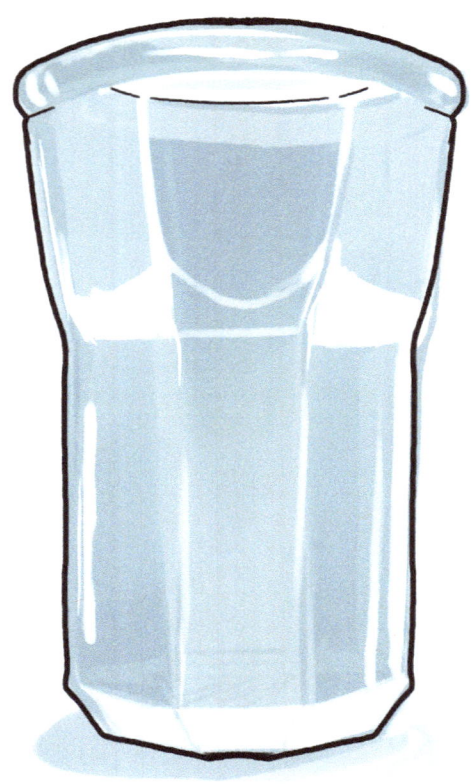

Cup

Dog

Dress

Fork

House

Keys

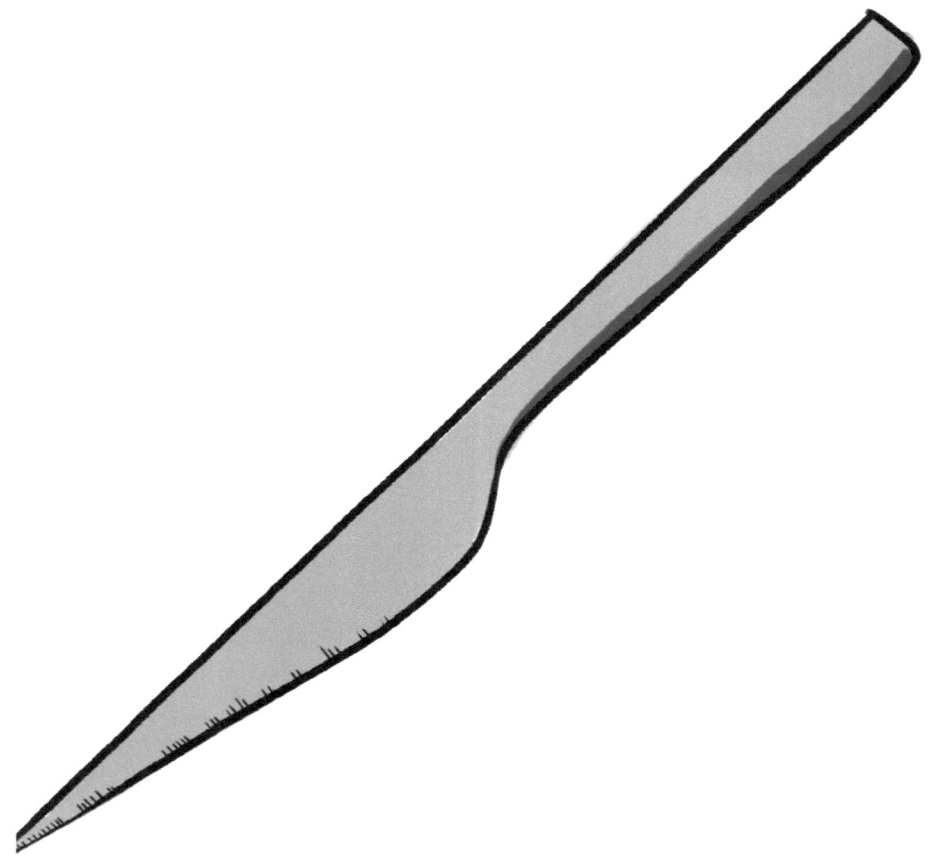

Knife

Lunch Bag

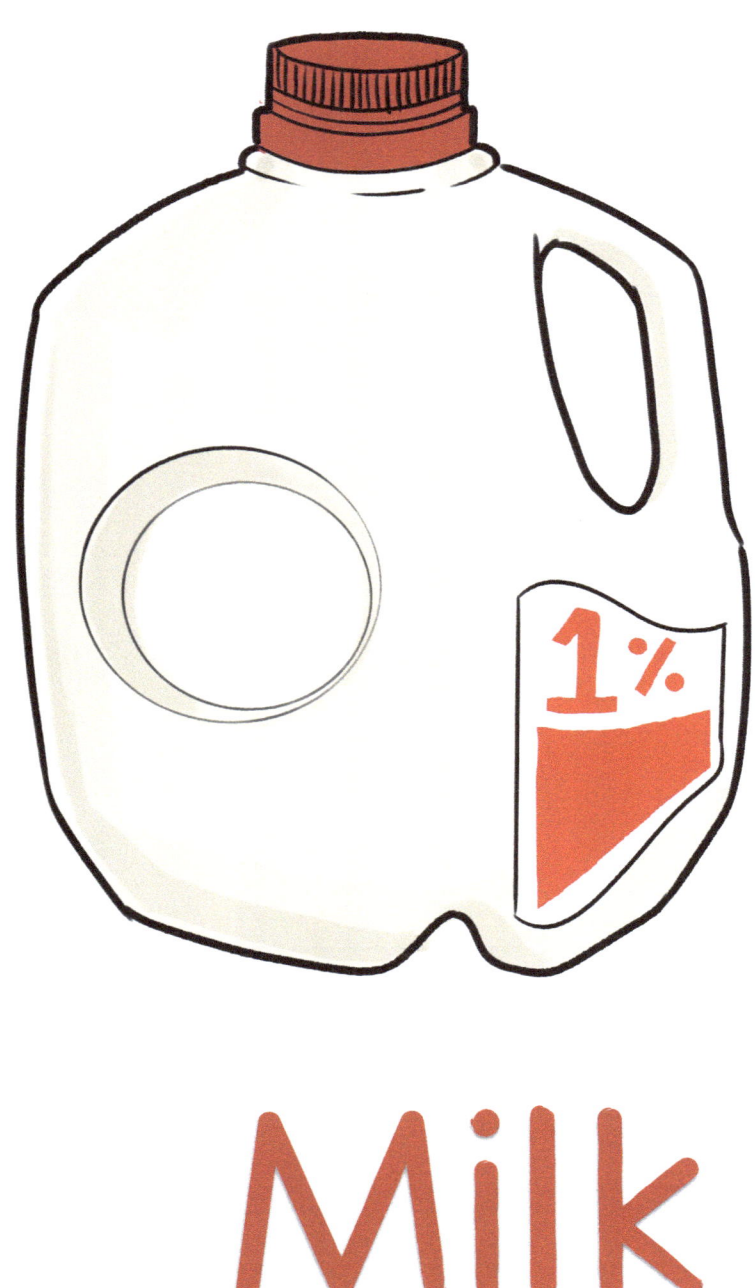

Milk

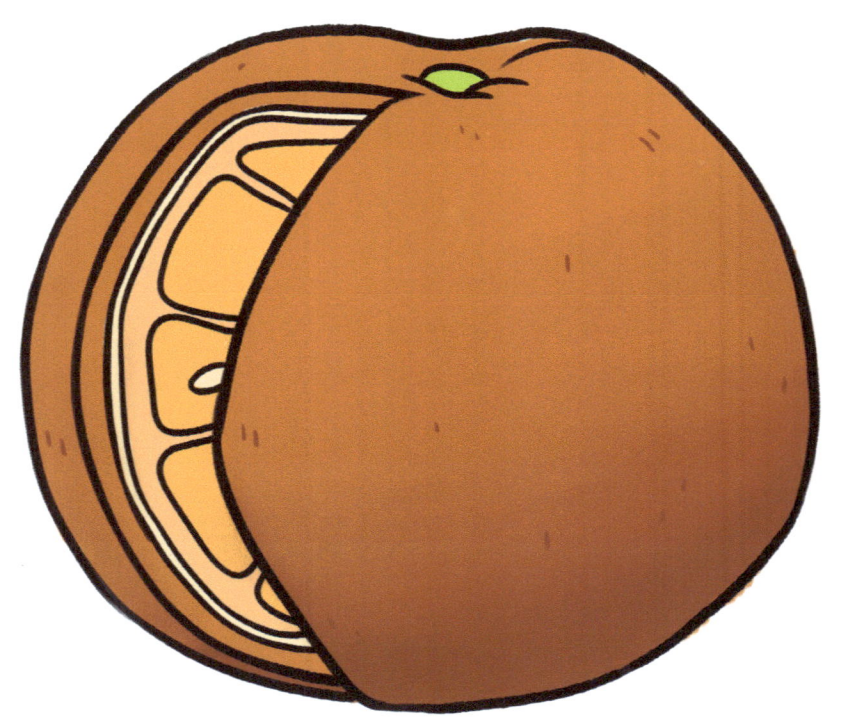

Orange

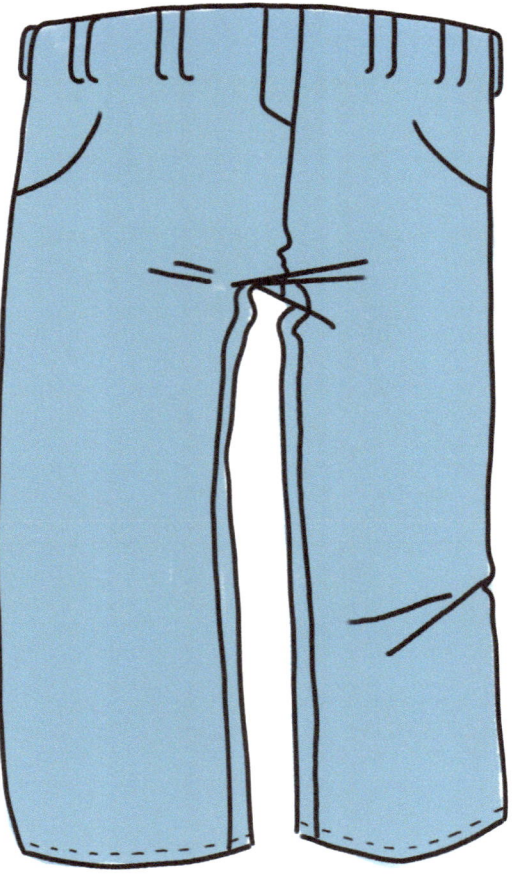

Pants

Pencils

Pillow

Soda

School Bus

Shoes

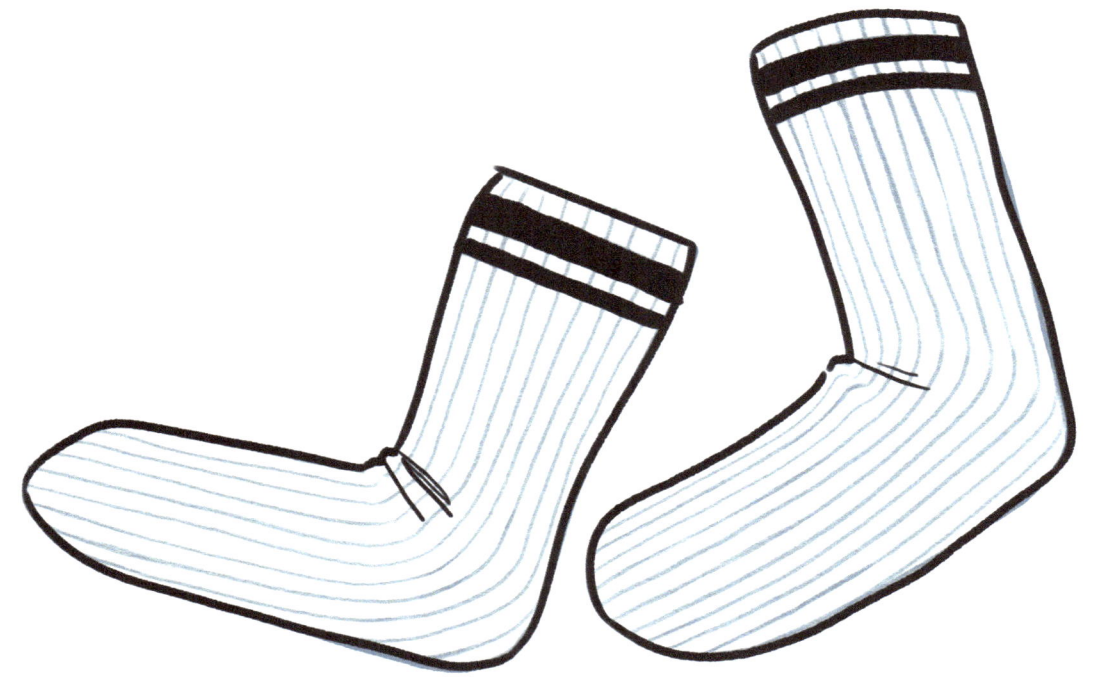

Socks

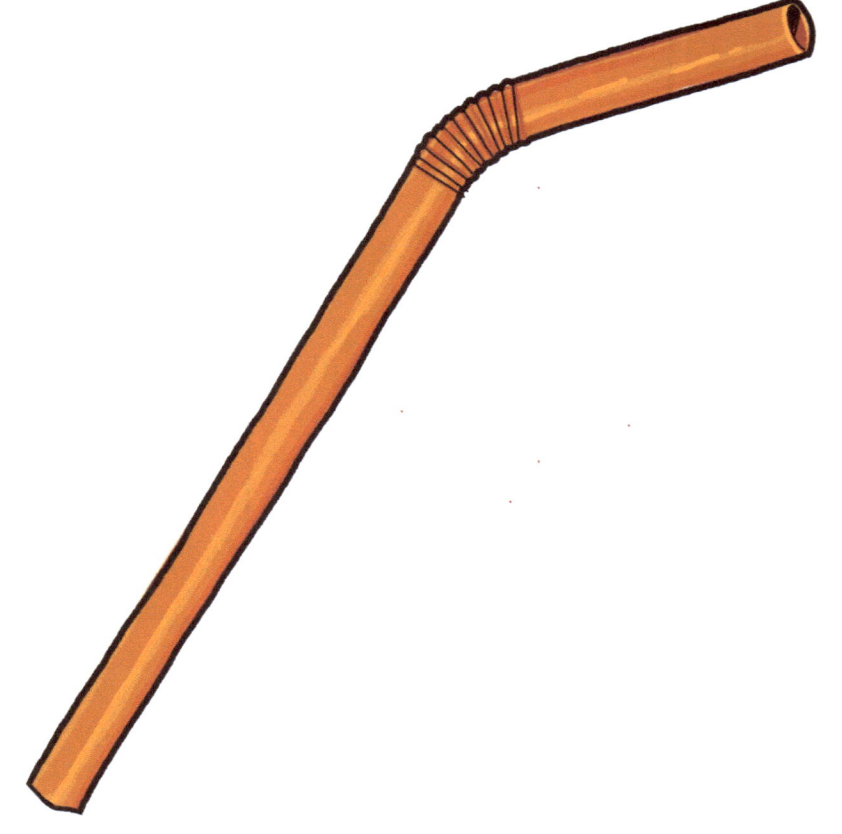

Straw

Table

Television

Locker

Tree

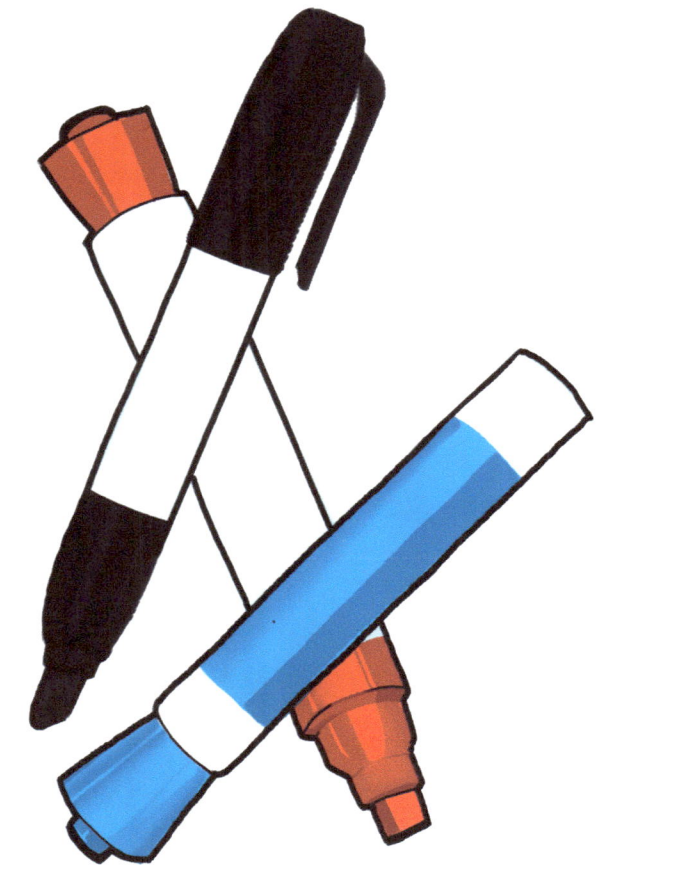

Markers

Desk

Whiteboard

Toothpaste

Water

Toothbrush

Reading Award

This certificate goes to:

_____

for reading "The Things We see"

Good Job!

More books, apps and resources at myskillsbooks.com

www.ingramcontent.com/pod-product-compliance
Lightning Source LLC
Chambersburg PA
CBHW042109090526
44592CB00004B/66